G Suit & Helmet Not Required!!

Phil Brewer & the '41 Chief

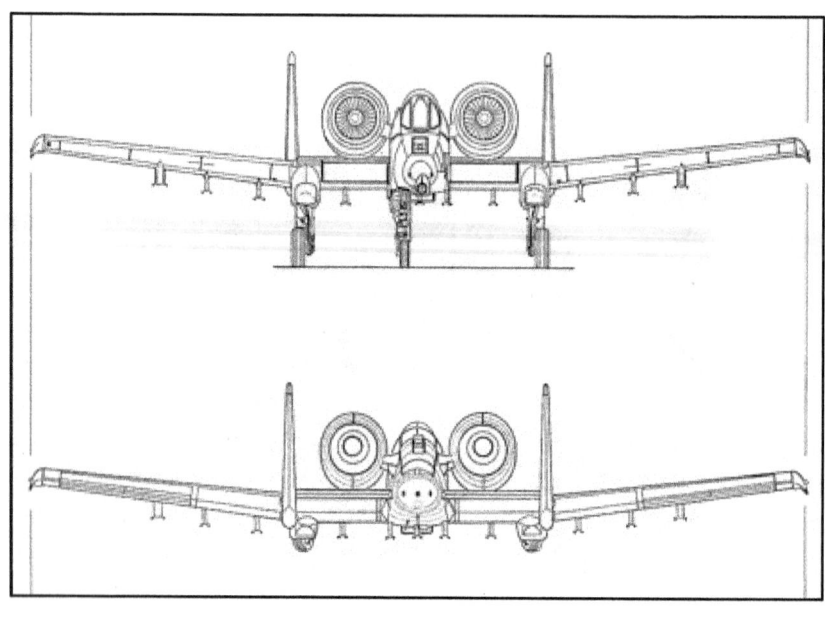

4 Secrets Of

Doing Business Like

A Fighter Pilot

www.philipbrewer.com

G Suit & Helmet Not Required!!

"Relic"

One day, I thought it would be fun to take my then, young, son, Aaron to the Pima Air Museum in Tucson Arizona. I proudly showed him all 4 airplanes that I had piloted while on active duty in the USAF. I even explained to him that 3 of the 4 I had actually flown that very plane.

A few seconds of silence ensued. Then, in his profound way, he asked me rhetorically, "Dad, doesn't that make you feel like a relic?"

Today, I am proud that I survived my time on active duty to become a relic and show my son what

I had done while serving my country in a very difficult time.

I dedicate this book to my incredible wife, Monica, my son, Aaron and his wife Mona, their 3 wonderful children - my Grandkids, Kaitlyn, Sarah and Aidan.

I also wish to remember the men with whom I served that didn't get the opportunity to be labelled a relic by their son. Rest in peace my comrades.

"When you have tasted flight, you will forever walk the earth with your eyes turned skyward, for there you have been, and there you will always long to return."

Leonardo de Vinci

www.philipbrewer.com

G Suit & Helmet Not Required!!

Introduction 9

Prologue - 'Man in the Flight Suit' 12

About Pilots: 17

Author Reflections 25

Introduce you to you! 29

The 4 Secrets then are: 32

Secret #1 Search out your Seed 33

Secret #2 Plant Your Seed! 61

Secret #3 Grow it!! 70

Sample Checklist (Affirmations): 77

Secret #4 Harvest Your Crop 96

Contact 101

Reviews and Endorsements: 102

Major Accomplishments: 106

"Once the wings go on, they never come off, whether they can be seen, or not. It fuses to the soul through adversity, fear and adrenaline and no one who has ever worn them with pride, integrity and guts, can ever sleep through the 'call of the wild' that wafts through bedroom windows in the deep of the night.

When a good pilot leaves the 'job' and retires, many are jealous, some are pleased and yet others, who may have already retired, wonder. We wonder if he knows what he is leaving behind, because we already know.

www.philipbrewer.com

G Suit & Helmet Not Required!!

We know, for example, that after a lifetime of camaraderie that few experience, it will remain as a longing for those past times.

We know in the world of flying, there is a fellowship which will last long after the flight suits are hung up in the back of the closet. We know even if he throws them away, they will be on him with every step and breath that remains in his life.

We also know how the very bearing of the man speaks of what he was and in his heart still is."
Author Unknown

"Success is not the key to happiness. Happiness is the key to success. If you love what you are doing, you will be successful." *Albert Schweitzer*

www.philipbrewer.com

Introduction

Why is my experience gained as a professional fighter pilot relevant to business and success as an entrepreneur? The discipline involved, as well as the dedication to excellence are enormous. Couple that with the willingness to learn extremely new skills and the ability to accept extreme challenges placed on mind and body.

These and many other important components are required to become an elite USAF pilot. These then are traits that have guided me in every endeavor I have pursued since.

Many professionals are surrounded by other similar professionals. The tendency is to forget how special they are. They tend to forget how others view them! This is equally true in the fighter pilot community.

Many of the lessons I learned later in life have taught me that anyone properly indoctrinated and made aware of their own life skills can adopt and learn these attitudes. That is what I will I teach you in this book.

While, by necessity, some experiences learned are best told in the form of the events as they unfolded, I ask you, the reader to enjoy the story and feel the feelings, that unless you have been there, can only be imagined. This book is not specifically a memoir. However, many of the best lessons in life are told through the real life event.

"If you can dream it, you can do it." Walt Disney

My belief is that as you read and re-read this book you will gain insight into your own

www.philipbrewer.com

G Suit & Helmet Not Required!!

special uniqueness. And with that insight you will be able to successfully grow your career in whatever endeavor you may choose.

"If one advances confidently in the direction of his dreams, and endeavors to live the life which he has imagined, he will meet with a success unexpected in common hours." Henry David Thoreau

Prologue - 'Man in the Flight Suit'

The air was blue, with those great big white puffy clouds. The feeling of the crisp morning air, tinged with the smell of the JP4 jet fuel was invigorating. Taxiing along in my A-7D Corsair II jet, sitting high above the pavement, on top of 14250 pounds of available thrust, I felt on top of the world!

I was strapped in to the jet, complete with a *Nomex* fire resistant flight suit, my helmet painted in squadron colors, a g-suit and oxygen mask. All of this was connected in an orchestrated manner to a seat that had a ballistic charge under my butt.

The g-suit is like a pair of chaps, tightly zippered around your legs and waist. A hose connects from an air source to bladders on the left side of the suit. The air is from very high pressure bleed air bypassed off the number 5 stage compressor of the motor.

The function of the g-suit is to flow pressurized air into the bladders and inflate. This causes a very high degree of pressure to be exerted on the legs and abdomen. It helps to prevent the blood from flowing out of the upper body in the legs, thus enabling you to stay 'conscious' while pulling up to 7+ g's.

www.philipbrewer.com

G Suit & Helmet Not Required!!

A "g" is a gravity. The best way to explain this is to think of your present weight. For example, if you weigh 200 pounds, then at 1g, or one gravity, you are feeling your normal body of 200 pounds. But at 2 g's, you are feeling the equivalent to your body of 200 x 2 or 400 pounds. A 3 g pull would feel like 600 pounds. And so on.

The ballistic charge under the seat is connected to a handle trigger that would shoot you and your seat up the rails and presumably separate you from a stricken aircraft. Located in the back of the seat is a parachute that will open automatically once a separate charge blasts you apart from the seat. Of course, this is after you exited the now unmanned aircraft.

The helmet is to keep you from knocking yourself out if you encounter turbulence and slam your head against the canopy. It is also to prevent head injury during an egress from the aircraft.

Strapped to the face of the helmet is a visor that functions to protect your eyes from the windblast of up to 500 mph should you have to eject. Additionally, the oxygen mask is connected to a source of oxygen that would mix with ambient air. It is also under pressure so you could continue to function up to as high as 50,000 feet, without passing out from lack of oxygen.

If this pressurized oxygen should disappear, you would be rendered helpless within seconds. That is because the oxygen in your lungs is being expelled out due to the total lack of any pressure at higher altitudes. This even if you were attempting to hold your breath!

"Ruckus flight, cleared for takeoff", rumbled the steady voice of the tower controller. "Roger, Ruckus cleared for takeoff" I respond. A silent hand signal to the wingman and we simultaneously lower our canopies as we finish our checklist. Next, we arm our seats, change our radios to tactical frequency and turn on our Identification Friend or Foe set (IFF for short). Our lights come on together and we taxi purposefully in formation onto the runway.

Lining up, I give the signal to my wingman, #2, to advance power. He nods acceptance of the command. Final check of the instruments and another silent signal with the head, we release brakes together. Another quick check of the wingman and then the runway ahead as we quickly accelerate down the runway.

We reach safety check speed, and I begin raising the nose slowly by pulling back on the control stick. Almost immediately, we break free of the bonds of gravity and begin our climb. A tap on my helmet, with a head jerk back signals the wingman to raise the gear and subsequently the flaps.

G Suit & Helmet Not Required!!

"Ruckus flight, cleared tactical", from the controller. Another signal and we changed to a predetermined battle tactical scenario, with radios, IFF and other switches. A quick 'waggle' of the rudder pedals "kicks" out my wingman into loose formation. We visually look each other over for problems, fluids leaking, bombs hanging poorly, etc.

When all satisfied, another 'waggle' and my wingman and we separate to 4000 feet apart. Then, pushing over our birds, we 'slither' down to a battle tactical altitude of about 100 feet above the surface of the earth.

This is just the beginning of the *'man in the flight suit'*. Each and every flight begins in very much the same way. Each and every time, hundreds of checks and rechecks, planning and executing, checking and more checking, while working in a natural way, maintaining a total sense of purpose and professionalism.

And sometimes, all the checks still weren't enough and someone didn't come home.

The point is, an attack fighter pilot is exceptionally capable, well trained and disciplined. Constantly thinking of scenarios in the here and now, as well as planning for events to unfold 5-10 minutes in the future. And at speeds of 7+ miles per minute, this requires thinking, planning and then acting now, to influence the outcome up to 70 miles away!

I began thinking of all the planning and training ingrained in me, and realized that these skills were useful to me in the execution of my first business.

As the years of activity and success went by, more and more I realized that our breed of man, that *'man in the flight suit'*, complete with g-suit and helmet, didn't need to have the advantage over someone without these skills.

That is, not if I were to provide him with the *secrets*! So in the brief pages that follow, I will provide you with the preliminary secrets of success that become inbred in the *'man in the flight suit'*.

With these secrets being employed, you may begin to acknowledge and enjoy the success in your personal endeavors. There are many similar types of endeavors for you that have become natural. This is similar to those of us trained to think ahead of the bird in time and distance.

www.philipbrewer.com

G Suit & Helmet Not Required!!

About Pilots:

(Adapted from countless email messages sent to me by other pilots and aspiring pilots. These points will greatly enhance your ability to think and act in business like a fighter pilot.)

1. As an aviator in flight you can do anything you want... As long as it's right... And we'll let you know if it's right after you get down!

2. You can't fly forever without getting killed!

3. As a pilot only two bad things can happen to you and one of them will.

- One day you will walk out to the aircraft knowing that it is your last flight in an airplane..

- One day you will walk out to the airplane not knowing that it is your last flight in an airplane..

4. Any flight over water in a single engine airplane will absolutely guarantee abnormal engine noises and vibrations.

5. There are Rules and there are Laws. The rules are made by men who think that they know better how to fly your airplane than you. The Laws (of Physics) were made by the Great One. You can, and sometimes should, suspend the Rules but you can never suspend the Laws.

6. More about Rules:

- The rules are a good place to hide if you don't have a better idea and the talent to execute it.

- If you deviate from a rule, it must be a flawless performance.   (e.g., If you fly under a bridge, don't hit the bridge.)

7. The pilot is the highest form of life on earth.

8. The ideal pilot is the perfect blend of discipline and aggressiveness.

9. About check rides:

G Suit & Helmet Not Required!!

- The only real objective of a check ride is to complete it and get the 'blankety blank' check airman out of your airplane.

- It has never occurred to any flight examiner that the examinee couldn't care less what the examiner's opinion of his flying ability really is.

10. The medical profession is the natural enemy of the aviation profession.

11. The job of the Wing Commander is to worry incessantly that his career depends solely on the abilities of his aviators to fly their airplanes without mishap and that their only minuscule contribution to the effort is to bet their lives on it.

12. Have you ever noticed that the only experts who decree that the age of the pilot is over are people who have never flown anything? Also, in spite of the intensity of their feelings that the pilot's day is over I know of no such expert who has volunteered to be a passenger in a non-piloted aircraft.

13. It is absolutely imperative that the pilot be unpredictable. Rebelliousness is very predict able. In the end, conforming almost all the time is the best way to be unpredictable.

14. He who demands everything that his aircraft can give him is a pilot; he that demands one iota more is a fool.

15. If you're gonna fly low, do not fly slow!

www.philipbrewer.com

G Suit & Helmet Not Required!!

16. About night flying:

- Remember that the airplane doesn't know that it's dark.

- On a clear, moonless night, never fly between the (refueling) tanker's lights.

- There are certain aircraft sounds that can only be heard at night.

- If you are going to night fly, it might as well be in the weather so you can double count your exposure to both hazards.

- Night formation is really an endless series of near misses in equilibrium with each other.

- You would have to pay a lot of money at a lot of amusement parks and perhaps add a few drugs, to get the same blend of psychedelic sensations as a single engine night weather flight.

17. One of the most important skills that a pilot must develop is the skill to ignore those things that were designed by non-pilots to get the pilot's attention.

18. At the end of the day, the controllers, ops supervisors, maintenance guys, weather guessers, and birds; they're all trying to kill you and your job is to not let them!

19. The concept of "controlling" airspace with radar is just a form of FAA (Federal Bureau of Aviation) sarcasm directed at pilots to see if they're gullible enough to swallow it. Or to put it another way, when's the last time the FAA ever shot anyone down? (The FAA really stands for Federal Aviation Administration).

20. Remember that the radio is only an electronic suggestion box for the pilot. Sometimes the only way to clear up a problem is to turn it off.

21. It is a tacit, yet profound admission of the preeminence of flying in the hierarchy of the human spirit, that those who seek to control aviators via threats always threaten to take one's 'wings' and not one's life. I guess that really shows which of the two is really most important to an aviator!

22. Mastering the prohibited maneuvers in the Manual is one of the best forms of aviation life insurance you can get.

23. A tactic done twice is a procedure.

G Suit & Helmet Not Required!!

24. The aircraft G-limits are only there in case there is another flight by that particular airplane. *If subsequent flights do not appear likely, there are no G-limits!*

25. One of the beautiful things about a single piloted aircraft is the quality of the social experience. (For non aviators it must be noted that most airplanes have two pilot seat positions).

26. If a mother has the slightest suspicion that her infant might grow up to be a pilot, she had better teach him to put things back where he got them!

The ultimate responsibility of the pilot is to fulfill the dreams of the countless millions of earthbound ancestors who could only stare skyward ...and wish.

"Life has no limitations, except the ones you make." Les Brown

www.philipbrewer.com

G Suit & Helmet Not Required!!

Author Reflections

As I write this, I pause to reflect upon the reasons for my success, within both my personal life and my business ventures. I have been fortunate to be able to take the techniques and skills I learned as a trained USAF A-7D and A-10A attack fighter pilot and successfully channel them into all other aspects of my life.

I never thought about the prospects of being self-employed and certainly did not envision being an entrepreneur; but circumstances moved me in that direction. Being a single seat jet pilot, fashioned me with the skills to tread confidently through life. I later realized that my successes were due in large part to that confidence.

Life has many facets. One very important key to success comes from how you work with it and control your attitude.

After making the transition from a fighter pilot to a business entrepreneur, I began to notice many similarities between the two that I had not considered previously. I correlated these experiences to my life growing up, as well as the wisdom gained from experience. However, I wondered how people perceived me as the *"Man in a Flight Suit"*.

Men in uniform have oft been revered in our society: soldiers, police, firemen, military personnel, and so forth. Perhaps it is because of their uniform that they stand out above the rest of society. And they are different from the rest. They are the sentinels of the sectors they represent in our society.

Take away the uniform and that sense of status seems to fade away as well, whether consciously or not. I wanted to be seen with that former perception all of the time, not just when I was in uniform. I wanted to continue to be that sentinel, and I realized that I could be.

With the seeming difference between the flight suit man and the non-flight suit man, I came to the realization that this difference didn't need to exist, at least not so drastically!

Trust me! You do not need to have been a single seat attack fighter pilot. Nor do you need a 'g' suit and helmet! You can take your past successes,

G Suit & Helmet Not Required!!

apply them, and begin moving forward in life in a major way with the attitude and mindset of *'A Man with a Flight Suit!'*

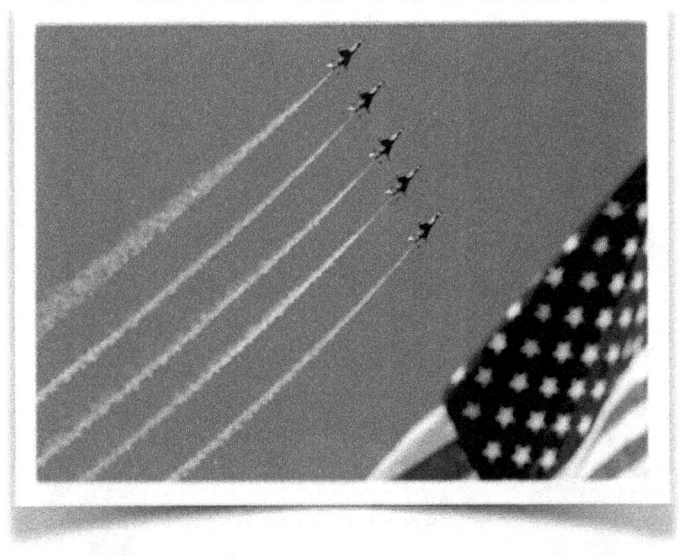

"Quality is not an act, it is a habit." Aristotle

"The difference between great people and everyone else is that great people create their lives actively, while everyone else is created by their lives - passively waiting to see where life takes them next. The difference between the two is the difference between living fully and just existing."

—Michael Gerber, The E-Myth Revisited

www.philipbrewer.com

Introduce you to you!
Is it time to meet you?
Go ahead, let's meet you!

I will prove to you in the next few pages that there is absolutely nothing that you can't do in your life.

Don't believe me?

Then read on.....*You can do or be anything in life! I know this to be a fact, beyond all reasonable doubt. I don't need to have ever met you or talked with you or in any way be acquainted with you. So, how can I make such a bold statement? It's simple!*

__I know that at some point in your life, you have already achieved something.__

Therefore, Seed your future from your past!

No matter what it was, you have already done something significant in your life for you. This thing, this event, occurrence or whatever 'it' was, might not have even been a noticed achievement to anyone else. But *you* know what 'it' is. You would love to brag about it to someone.

Anyone, if given the chance would love to talk about 'it'. Whatever 'it' is or was. This 'it' is your seed. The only one you need to have. In the next few pages, we will, together, you and I, find it, plant it, fertilize it, and grow it.

It is an absolute law of nature and God that all growth comes initially from a seed that has already been given to you and is in existence. In life, you must become the farmer for that seed, and replant your garden in any area of the world you wish to conquer.

The 4 Secrets then are:

1. *Search out your seed,*

2. *Plant it,*

3. *Grow it,*

4. *Harvest your crop.*

"The will to win, the desire to succeed, the urge to reach your full potential... these are the keys that will unlock the door to personal excellence."
Confucius

www.philipbrewer.com

G Suit & Helmet Not Required!!

Secret #1 Search out your Seed.

I need you to go way back in your memory bank. This is crucial. Try and remember your first really big accomplishment? The thing to keep in mind is that there is something you have accomplished. Or perhaps, many 'somethings'. For some of us, it's very obvious. For others, we have to dig. This is especially true if you have had an upbringing that might not have been positive or up-lifting.

Your something or accomplishment, could have been an event like going out for little league, or trying out to be a cheerleader. You might have been asked to be in a school play. This event might even have terrified you! But for some reason, you did try out, and you were selected for a part in the play.

I made it on to a little league team. I also was forced to take piano lessons. What is the relevance? Well, little league in my mind was manly, but piano was for sissies.   No offense. That is how I saw it then. But no matter. They both required practice. And persistence.

"Things don't happen. They are made to happen." John F Kennedy

You couldn't just show up one time and get on the team. Practice, discipline and more practice. You couldn't just go to the lessons in piano.

Eventually, I got good enough to play regularly in baseball, and even hit a home run. It was a very small thing in retrospect. But, then again, maybe not really so small.

You see, that little victory, for me, meant I could accomplish something. It was something that required me to stretch and to work beyond me by becoming something else. It allowed me to see me in a different perspective.

www.philipbrewer.com

G Suit & Helmet Not Required!!

Learning to play piano was also like that. Even though I disliked it, I kept doing it because I was disciplined to do so. Eventually, I memorized some pieces and actually got through them at a very small, public recital. What a feat that was for me at the time, to succeed at something I had once thought was just for sissies!

Are you getting the idea? Take this moment, and identify some early seeds of your success from early on in your life. Observe the progression of these early childhood memories. If you were a guy, it might have been an after-school fight or learning how to ice skate or climb a tree on your own. You see, these early victories were common place for you, weren't they?

School for me was such a drag! I only wanted to be outside playing in the fresh air. So, being in a class room all day sitting and trying to concentrate and focus felt like punishment to me! But still, there were the little achievements. The grades you didn't think you could make or the papers you wrote.

I found a paper recently, probably written when I was in 8th grade at Drake Junior High School, in Arvada, Colorado. Maybe it was 7th, at (long ago closed) Wheelus US Air Force Base,

Tripoli, Libya. No matter. The topic of the paper was actually to write whatever came into our heads as we listened to music. Even still today, I like what I had written. And so did my teacher. I was encouraged.

"Believe you can and you are halfway there." Theodore Roosevelt

I could run fast as well. I remember being encouraged to run in track. So, I did. Again, a little thing, but I could compete. I was also always wrestling with my brothers and sister. So, it was no big deal for me when I made the wrestling team. And I did very well.

When I was 14, I went after school and got a job as a bus boy at a Furr's Cafeteria. I made my own money. Wow, was that great. And, again, what had I done? I had scored another little victory. I began having a veritable little pile of them.

"*Be careful the environment you choose for it will shape you; be careful the friends you choose for you will become like them.*" W. Clement Stone

Are you starting to get the idea? Take the time now to really delve in to some of your early and special memories. It's ok to forget the bad stuff. You don't need that anyhow. It is not productive and certainly no longer important. Your future successes will more easily be a result of you focusing on some of the more significant little achievements.

Between my sophomore and junior year in High School, the family moved from Arvada, Colorado to Great Falls, Montana. It was really tough to move so frequently. But again, 'little' people, if properly encouraged, can be very resilient. Mom and Dad helped my older brother and me get a summer job at a sheep ranch in northern Idaho. We lived in a bunk house, like real cowboys.

"Small dreams attract small people. Big dreams attract big people!!" Dave Menninger.

I had already learned the importance of hard work. But, I didn't like to save money. Mom said it burned a hole in my pocket. I took that literally, I think. So, I bought stuff. One of the first items I bought was a ten speed bicycle. I have no recollection today of what 'useful' things I did with money, but I had a job. And that gave me a feeling of Importance and self worth.

That summer, in Idaho, I learned to drive the ranch truck. It was a three speed with the shift on the column. (Also known then as three on a tree!) You know, with a clutch and all. I never remember telling anyone I couldn't do it. I just did it.

I learned how to operate a very large tractor with a 10 foot cutting blade. It had little triangular blades, and when those blades broke they would need replacing. I would hop off the tractor, get out my tools and a new blade and begin to replace the damaged one.

I know it doesn't sound like much, but, believe me these types of accomplishments are huge. And, you also have them. These little miracles of early accomplishment. Are you getting the idea? Ok then, what similar accomplishments can you recall? Stop now and make your list:

1. What was one of your first really big achievements? What effect did it have?

2. Recall your first athletic achievement. Did you realize at the time how it was part of your building block for future successes?

3. List one of your first memorable school achievements? (For me, getting C's and above on my report card meant a lot).

4. List the first time you earned money: (Not an allowance, but a return of monetary reward for something you produced).

What about let downs or put downs? Do these factor in? Of course they do. However, really, if you think about it, why should they? So many people let a single little failure, put down or let down completely change their life. It might have been some careless little remark that meant nothing. But you let it mean everything. Why do you let someone else's inadequacies, through their remarks, change your wonderful life?

Let's spend just a little bit of time on this. Who are/were these people? A casual friend, a relative, maybe even an important relative? Like a Mom or Dad? Maybe it was a total nobody. Someone who just barely passed through your life.

G Suit & Helmet Not Required!!

"No one can hurt you without your consent." Eleanor Roosevelt.

Why do we allow that one person to totally control our life? You see, you have the ability to control whether or not to allow this person's input to relegate you to a third class position. And, it impacts everything - your allowance of *their* thoughts about you. Get it again. *Your allowance*....

You *allowed*... So since *you* allow, then only allow those things which build you. Because ultimately, you are the best in the world at whatever you decide to do. You just need to believe that. You should really get serious about becoming your own person. Your own unique, totally individual beautiful person.

And the way to believe that is for you to lock on to or anchor your other successes. A real success would be best. It could even be fantasized.

Besides 'reality'! [Reality?] Who really knows reality?

No one, not even you knows reality. Your perception of your reality of the situation and how you accept it is the final word on the subject.

[Repeat that.] ...... *Your perception of your reality of the situation and how you accept it is the final word on the subject!!!*

www.philipbrewer.com

G Suit & Helmet Not Required!!

"Failures in our minds are like a poison, but the repetition of our successes is the antidote. And the only way to do that is to keep getting up and going at it again."
Phil Brewer

In all honesty my 'little successes' kept me moving forward. Therefore, in your life, when you doubt yourself, a reminder of these little successes are your encouragements! Encouragements for moving into the realm of being truly great in some particular way.

Now, let's get one other thing straight. Take these victories and move to the next victory circle.

Don't just replay this one single little incident and let it become your life.

"High expectations are the key to everything." Sam Walton

How many people have allowed a single success to become their future? They didn't build to the next level. They stopped right there. They simply became the next person at the water-cooler who bragged about something to everyone and never, ever did another thing again.

So, of course, this is not the result you want. You allow this incident to define your next triumph, your next little Waterloo. Move on. Repeat your last triumph in a new arena. Build on it!

www.philipbrewer.com

G Suit & Helmet Not Required!!

So, how do you climb the next hurdle? First, you must move forward. Find your next mountain to climb and then when you have doubts or inhibitions, *just play back your last success!*

"You can't build a reputation on what you are going to do!"
Henry Ford

I am astonished how little we achieve in our life because we don't do this. And worse is how easily we allow someone else to define normal or average. And then we go fit in that small little box.

We start something new and immediately, we either seek to find out what is required, or what is normal. And rather than find our own standard, since we don't know what that is, we set our standard against others.

We're like the sales guy who looks around at what everyone else is selling and who is doing the best, and we 'fit in.' We attempt to beat the race times of those who are wonderful at their sport. We should rather just go full out at our own pace.

There are many stories of people who have entered a new field of endeavor. An endeavor in which success is calculated by how many, or how fast or both, a task is completed.

This person, not knowing what the standard of excellence has been, is doing their job as they believe they should, only to discover they are lauded as top in their department or company. And then something happens. They begin to fit into the 'standard' and slide into a 'normal' level, usually of mediocrity. And this level is far below what they had initially accomplished.

Other examples of this might be coming into a new job and either asking what is expected in terms of production, or being told what is expected.

G Suit & Helmet Not Required!!

Maybe a commission or bonus is paid when a certain dollar level per month is achieved.

So, this bonus level is hit and exceeded by mere pennies. What if the level was increased by 20%, and this becomes the one required to get the bonus? Then, what seemed impossible becomes possible.

"Adventure can be had at anytime. It just depends on your state of mind." Clive Cussler

It has been said that the game of golf, since Tiger Woods began playing, has become even more competitive and played at an even higher level. The reason? Because Tiger Woods, unlike most competitors, really only competes against himself. He sets his own standard without regard to what his competition is doing.

Another example of this would be to look at the world records set 40 years ago. Today, they are broken fairly routinely by high school age athletes.

I have seen this in my life was when I was selected to go to pilot training. Ever since first becoming a pilot in the USAF, I have heard people tell me that that was what they truly wanted to do. Then they would offer some explanation as to why they didn't.

Here is an example of this, "Well, I couldn't get accepted because of my eyes."

I responded with, "Really, what was wrong with your eyes?"

"Well, I wore glasses, and I heard that if you wore glasses, you couldn't be a pilot."

So, here it is. They decided on their own they couldn't qualify, based on what they thought they knew, but not on what they found out by actually trying.

www.philipbrewer.com

G Suit & Helmet Not Required!!

In retrospect it's funny, since I too actually wore glasses. However, prior to the requisite military eye test, I ate carrots for a week or so and my Mom prayed for me!

It didn't really surprise me that I passed the requisite test the required number of times - once. Because I *attempted* and because I *decided* to pass the test.

What is the lesson? Don't allow yourself to be the 'crab in the bucket' with others who are determined to set the bar low enough that they don't ever have to achieve their greatness.

You know about the crab in the bucket, right? If not, here is the analogy. Essentially, if you want a crab to stay in an open bucket, it is impossible to do that without a lid. So the fix? Simply drop another crab in with the first crab. Whenever one tries to get out, the other pulls it down.

This is as good a time as any to hit this point hard. I know that for me, the absolute best performance I can give on anything is to be around those who encourage me. We must, absolutely *must,* surround ourselves with those who build us up. If you cannot, you have to find a way to change your environment so that this can happen.

What was your favorite subject in school? Chances are, you are doing what you do today because you excelled in something that you were encouraged in. Sure, there are exceptions. But, even if you wanted to move into something that was of interest to you, you had to get encouragement somewhere.

So, seek encouraging situations and people. Challenge yourself to race against yourself, but move in the direction of being encouraged by others.

Unfortunately today, many schools are staffed by negative teachers and administrators. It no longer seems they are in the business of creating excellence. So, you will need to overcome some of the negative mindsets that are most assuredly imbedded.

This is best accomplished with the help of a coach. Someone who knows you well enough and can challenge you to do and be your best! Someone who will help you aspire to reach higher.

My first experience with this was as a cook in a very large restaurant. The owner and the head chef constantly gave me reasons to want to excel. They complimented me in terms that meant something to me. This encouraged me to rise even higher and work even harder.

One of my biggest challenges ever involved a mentor experience. I was stationed at Vance AFB, Oklahoma. The pilot training program was exceptionally demanding and challenging. To worsen matters, the instructor assigned to take me from being a freshly minted officer to skilled pilot was quite simply awful.

"Always do your best. What you plant now, you will harvest later." Og Mandino

His ability to inspire confidence did not exist. He had a lackluster attitude towards me, his charge. Further, he had absolutely no desire to be an instructor pilot.

Since I hadn't developed my own dreams and goals, I struggled. I didn't really know myself. In retrospect, I allowed his poor attitude to take away the opportunity in front of me to be a jet pilot

www.philipbrewer.com

G Suit & Helmet Not Required!!

My solution? I decided to simply quit. No kidding! I didn't want to work that hard for something that didn't have any meaning to me. I didn't aspire to be what he was.

"It is always too early to quit." Norman Vincent Peale

In order to quit, I was required to meet with the Chief Of Training. He wanted to know why I was in Pilot Training in the first place. I really didn't have any answer. I had never thought about it!

He proceeded to berate me. He reminded me of the difficulty of even being there. Angrily, he informed me how I was wasting the slot. There were many other men that would have loved to have had my position.

He appropriately called me a wimp for my reasons and decision. Somehow this talk motivated me!

I began to realize that my position was really worth fighting for. Abruptly, as he was ready to throw me out, I asked him if I could possibly get another shot.

To this day I am not sure why I got another chance. It really shouldn't have happened. He carefully explained the consequences of what I had attempted to do, and then arranged for me to be placed conditionally with another instructor.

This different instructor, Lt 'Roach' Jones was a true lover of the art of mentoring. Roach helped to change my life. He not only was a good pilot, he also made learning to fly great fun. Every day I worked harder to not only succeed for my goal, but also to succeed for him.

G Suit & Helmet Not Required!!

"Choice, not chance, determines one's destiny." Unknown

I now know that this kind of mentorship and leadership is crucial to most endeavors. I strongly believe this to be true. Therefore, I suggest, you must force yourself to get out there and find your inspirational mentor. Work at it. (Interestingly, Roach graduated his three students at the top of the class. Thank you Roach Jones!!)

Before I was given that second chance to stay on in pilot training, my goal was simply to get into the USAF. I had a pregnant wife and needed the income and benefits. Past that, I didn't have much motivation.

I hadn't wanted to be a pilot badly enough to be challenged by a poor mentor. I hadn't made it my dream. It wasn't important enough for me to fight for the prize.

Now, I simply *had* to be a jet pilot. I further determined I needed to be a fighter jock! It no longer was an option. Since I now had a true mentor who encouraged me, the work necessary to accomplish this new goal was secondary.

Was it hard work? Oh yes, *definitely*. Beyond belief. I hadn't sought any challenging technical courses in college, so I had to learn all kinds of very technical skills. Mathematics, weather, flight planning, navigation, memory skills, as well as other things I've long forgotten.

G Suit & Helmet Not Required!!

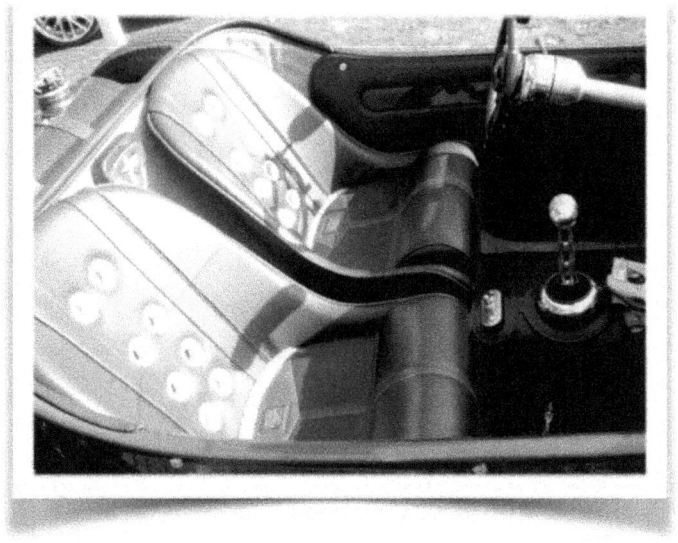

"It doesn't take any more effort to dream a big dream than it does to dream a small dream!!" Leslie Clark.

So, a quick word about dreams and goals. For most of us, a dream is a wish, a goal is a destination. Whatever you wish for is simply that. You set your goals based on your dreams. So, in identifying your goals, first think about the 'perfect' life for you.

Consider areas in your life - spiritual, relationship, type of home, car, how many kids, etc. And then, based on this list of important items, identify what you actually want to achieve in increments of 1 year, 5 years and 10 years.

For me, I have a goal to make a certain income. Then I break this down into what I will pursue to make that income. Next, I identify the specific steps needed and actions required to achieve those goals.

Think of it as if you are deciding to take a journey to some exotic and far off place. If it is reachable over land, then you have choices to make. You could walk, skate board, bicycle, drive, hitchhike, fly, take a train.

Well, you get the idea! You have to judge the time frame and the distance. Obviously, you can't possibly decide to walk if you have to go 2000 miles, and you want to do it within 10 days! So the vehicle has to match the result.

With goals regarding income, if you have never made $250,000 per year, and your present income is $75,000, you are going to have to identify some radical changes in what you are presently doing to achieve this new level. You must always be willing to make changes. Sacrifice will be part of the price.

G Suit & Helmet Not Required!!

"Believe in yourself! Have faith in your abilities! Without a humble but reasonable confidence in your own powers you cannot be successful or happy." Norman Vincent Peale

So, now when you have the vehicle in mind, begin planning the journey, step by step. You have identified your destination, so you only need to begin! This is the key to goal setting. You begin by first writing down the goal/destination, then, look at the elements required.

We have all seen people pursue an education to be an engineer or whatever, and then they discover that not only do they not like the work, but it doesn't make them the income that fits their dreams.

This is why coaching and mentoring are so important. You want to do what you love and enjoy, what you are called to do, but also, that which rewards you appropriately to fit your dreams.

"Do not let what you cannot do interfere with what you can do." *John Wooden*

www.philipbrewer.com

G Suit & Helmet Not Required!!

"Don't judge each day by the harvest you reap but by the seeds that you plant." Robert Louis Stevenson

Secret #2 Plant Your Seed!

Planting your seed is all about taking what we have discussed regarding finding your past achievement and putting it in the best area to grow.

In the first chapter, we discussed the aspect of discovering your seed and laying out a plan on creating your future. So how is this accomplished? This seed planting?

First, we need to discover where to plant the seed. This is where the idea of faith comes in so strongly. Faith is a term often used to discuss spiritual or religious aspects of life. Of course, there is a spiritual aspect to creating a new you.

The faith to which I am referring is exactly like that which allows you to expect a crop of vegetables after planting vegetable seeds. You expect that once the seeds are planted, and properly cared for, they will produce. This can be based on either your experience of this process, or the knowledge of someone else's experience.

So, this is the faith you need to have here. You need to understand that if you haven't used this technique, then rely on the experiences of someone else to guide you.

To work and grow, a vegetable seed doesn't need to be believed! This is also true of a mental, visualized seed. It doesn't hurt, but the seed will grow based on the nature of God's laws, just like gravity works. You don't have to believe in it for it to work. The faith aspect is in taking the action and planting the seed!

Begin planting your seed by visualizing your success. Do this with as much reality as you can muster. See as closely as possible in your mind (as if you were actually looking at it), that for which you are aiming....

Long before I became interested in reading for personal improvement and development, I had occasion to need to visualize. Visualization is a process of seeing in your mind the desired result before you have experienced it in the present or in a 'physical' realm.

Having made it through pilot training, water survival, basic mountain and winter survival, advance fighter training, then through four months of specialty training in the very complex single seat attack fighter, the A-7D, I hit a wall!

One of the requirements to successful completion of the course was to refuel behind an airborne tanker at night. If we didn't do it at least once, we would be washed out of the program. We were allowed two attempts.

We had already refueled during the day so it should have been a pretty easy process to do the same thing in the dark. The difference in this case happened to be the instructor - much more so than the event.

There were three students and one instructor. The instructor happened to be a very angry and arrogant senior squadron commander. His method of encouragement was to begin uttering obscenities well before we even got close to the tanker. "You idiots, we are getting ready to wash you out as fighter pilots, so let's go up and get this over with..." No kidding.

I had to overcome his lack of faith and create my own. Somewhere I had heard that you could go and 'arm chair' fly a mission. Arm chair flying is another way of saying to visualize.

It is sitting in a chair, and 'flying' the entire mission from you chair in your mind! I determined this was going to be a very important flight the next day. I was not ready to give up, roll over and 'wet on myself.' (This is an impolite way of saying giving up).

G Suit & Helmet Not Required!!

"Affirmation without discipline is the beginning of delusion." Jim Rohn

So I decided to try this suggested technique. I actually prefer to use the term 'arm chair' flying, because it sounds more logical than visualization. Again, it is just going through the motions of a future planned event.

Your goal is to see every aspect of the event, its potential dilemmas, hurdles, and such, and see yourself dealing with these potential problems in advance, before you actually deal with them for 'real'.

To think through a flight and see every detail of the flight from takeoff to landing was new to me.

However, I was told by an instructor to try doing this. So, I took the action and did exactly that. For over two hours each, three times, I visualized my flight the next night. That was my method of studying. I 'saw' every aspect of the flight.

The next evening, the same flight of four sleek A-7D aircraft found us rolling down the runway at 120 miles per hour. Flying in formation, the lights of my fighter gently caressed the night air. The aircraft acceleration steadily increased as we sped down the runway.

Within seconds, we reached nose rotation speed. Pulling back on the control stick, my aircraft began ever so gently to achieve a 12-degree nose up attitude.

Almost as soon as we did, we were airborne. The flight leader signaled gear up, flaps up and power back. 'Kicking' me from close formation to route or extended formation, we began to wait for our other flight element of two aircraft to join us. About three minutes later we had them in formation and began to set up on the climb to the pre-planned flight route.

G Suit & Helmet Not Required!!

"Be a yardstick of quality. Some people aren't used to an environment where excellence is expected." Steve Jobs

Forty minutes later, we reached the area to rendezvous with the flying gas station and were cleared in to join up with the tanker. Being a very dark night, it was easy to pick out this mammoth flight monster. It was a KC-135 and was all lit up like a giant flying Christmas tree.

Our flight lead screamed some obscenities at us, saying he wanted to get his gas before his rookies 'crashed' into the tanker and kept him dry (without fuel). Of course, all these intimidations were no longer of any validity to me, as I had already seen myself doing this very successfully many times in the past twenty four hours.

Interestingly, we all three {students} got our gas without troubles this time.

The point is:

1. See yourself doing successfully whatever it is you plan to accomplish.

2. Practice, practice, practice.

3. Never doubt yourself.

4. Above all, take action. Even the smallest action will empower you and move you forward. You cannot steer a parked car! You cannot take off an airplane until you apply power. The defining attribute to action is motion. Move forward now, this very minute. Let your preparation become your initial action.

Just - *Be* the success you were designed to be.

G Suit & Helmet Not Required!!

"The quality of a person's life is in direct proportion to their commitment to excellence, regardless of their chosen field of endeavor." Vince Lombardi

"Change your thoughts and you change your world." Norman Vincent Peale

Secret #3 Grow it!!

Decide to be the greatest expert in your field or endeavor!

Whatever business endeavor you choose to be associated with, make it your game to be the best. Not just good at something. Not just above average. But the greatest!

www.philipbrewer.com

G Suit & Helmet Not Required!!

How do you do this? You simply decide to label yourself as the greatest. As you admit it to yourself and to others, several very important things begin to happen for you.

First, you admit it to you! You cement in your mind and in your core, your belief of being confidently aware of your greatness. Your expert status! This translates itself in everything you do. Your actions become motivated by this inner knowledge that you are the best!!

And second, you are talking to others who may or may not be expert in anything. And if they are, they will respect your positioning of yourself. If they are not, they will most likely be in awe of meeting a true expert. To them, you represent in life that which they would appreciate having for themselves.

Being really good at something is truly rare and remarkable. (Think for a moment of someone you have met in your life who was an expert at something. Now try remembering if you ever met someone who was known by themselves or others as the worlds greatest!)

These same people, of course, by proximity to you, can enjoy being in the company of an expert and thereby gain a bit of their own notoriety. The notoriety of telling their friends that they met an expert in the field of _____!

Another big part of 'growing it' is having faith. You wouldn't plant a tomato seed in the ground and either not expect the seed to grow or expect it to grow something besides tomatoes! Often, people are actually doing what they need to be doing, but they doubt their actions, thus spoiling the crop. If you have the faith in your actions and don't doubt your work, you can certainly expect the correct results.

Let's review. An element that follows through all your steps is a process called visualization. You probably have not ever thought about this as a very young child, But as you grow older, you have to really get this element firmly entrenched in your habits.

Why? Because you have setbacks. You have little defeats. You have the occasional failure!!

So perceptibly, we start to see the failures in any attempt to move forward. This can almost certainly only lead to another failure. And then that becomes the new reality.

www.philipbrewer.com

G Suit & Helmet Not Required!!

"Discipline is the bridge between goals and accomplishment." Jim Rohn

If this has happened, it can be reversed - for sure. However, you must begin to exercise a different mindset. One in which you only allow yourself to see the event you are beginning with a successful conclusion.

Remember, you can begin to create your own reality. That reality you are creating must begin with you seeing the successful completion of an event. I recommend you do this multiple times a day, in many ways.

Further, become an expert at talking to yourself out loud. I compare this to you being your own cheerleader. Hear your voice actually commending you on your victory.

Guard your thoughts and mind from ever admitting anything less than perfection. It is better to not say anything if you cannot prevent yourself from speaking defeat or negativity. About anything, ever!! *Flee from gossipers*. Do not allow yourself to be anywhere that you can be mentally soiled.

One of the analogies of this book dwells on the Biblical principles of seed time and harvest. If you have ever grown a garden, you know that there are basic elements to a garden. A gardener never plants just one seed.

You would always guard and protect your new fragile plant. Since you planted it, you want it to grow. Therefore, you would guard and protect it. You would water it, weed it, and tend to it.

Think of these elements while you are reading. When I say flee from gossipers, use the common sense approach of protecting the soil and the seed. You wouldn't expect to gain much of a harvest if you routinely poured bleach or some other poison on your ground. In fact, you could kill your plant.

G Suit & Helmet Not Required!!

Every aspect of your successful journey must be viewed with this kind of concern and caution.

If you have developed a habit of negative talk or being around negative talk, that definitely needs to be changed. But you will have to work at it. And I do mean really work. An immediate requirement to change this habit is to write down a dozen affirmations on a card. These affirmations affirm the goals you wrote earlier. But they also may contain specific traits and habits that support your overall well being.

Carry them with you, and read them out loud to yourself, at least six times per day. The more you do it the better, but at least six times per day. Put a copy in the visor of your car, and every time you start your car, pull them down and recite them out loud. Reading them with great regularity is very important.

Write down affirmations that are a positive reflection of what you desire or what it is that you seek to change. Make it just like you are reading a checklist. Whenever we got in to pilot a plane in the USAF this was standard practice.

We would read the checklist, out loud, step-by-step, to make sure that we accomplished every required, seemingly mundane point. You could easily forget things, which missed could easily and quickly kill you.

In an airplane with a crew of two pilots, this reading was accomplished with a challenge and response technique. If you routinely drive with a spouse, try doing it in this manner.

This would make your affirmations take on an even bigger significance and relevance. However, in a single seat environment, you must concentrate and focus on the points. Try this. Focus on what you are saying as you are saying them. See it coming true.

Therefore, a 'checklist in your car', (your affirmations) - are a true reflection of a pilots normal routine.

www.philipbrewer.com

G Suit & Helmet Not Required!!

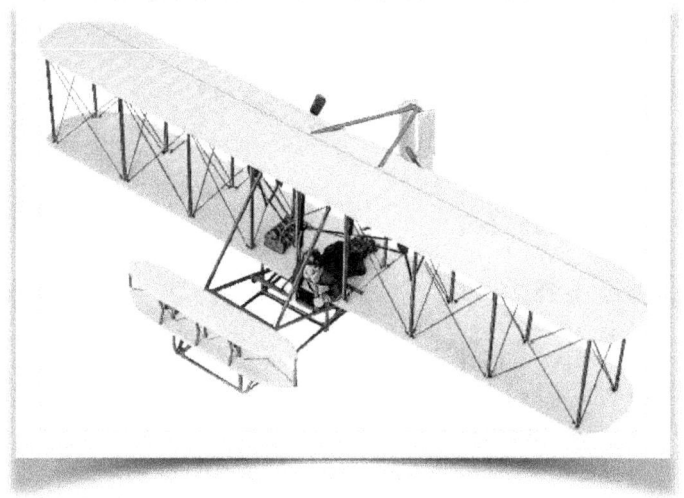

A. Huxley was quoted as saying, "Words are magical in the way they affect the minds of those who use them...."

Sample Checklist (Affirmations):

1) I am a winner!

2) I am in great health! (Say this even if you don't feel well. Never, ever say I don't feel well. Ever!)

3) I enjoy phenomenal success in all areas of my life.

4) I have a great spouse.

5) I have wonderful children.

6) I make $30,000 per month.

7) People are attracted to me.

8) I look great.

9) I am a great leader.

10) I am a great teacher.

11) I weigh 185.

12) I have tremendous energy.

13) I am enthusiastic and full of natural excitement.

"I always imagined I could be what I wanted to be." Chris Brown

www.philipbrewer.com

G Suit & Helmet Not Required!!

The secrets to effective self-talk, should include what you want to have, as if you already possess it. It should therefore always be in the *present tense*. It is best to be repeated out loud. You should say it with as much conviction as you can muster, until it becomes easier to say, naturally and with gusto.

Benefits include, but are not limited to, effectively changing your outlook on the day and your life, as well as perpetrating the actions necessary to put you on autopilot.

That's correct, autopilot. Your mind and your actions will begin to automatically drive you forward in the directions you have set for yourself.

Everything about our lives is traceable to our beliefs and perceptions. We literally are in charge of creating ourselves. If you only accept the notion of this, without even totally embracing the concept, you will move forward.

"Self suggestion makes you master of yourself." W. Clement Stone

The last couple of direct things I will say about affirmations relates to an experience I had getting ready for my Federal Aviation Administration, FAA, Airline Transport Pilot (ATP) test.

I had completed my obligation with the USAF and was preparing for a possible career with the airlines. The ATP test is a very long and exhaustive test. The average pass score after studying for months is 73. And this was on the second attempt.

I had purchased a study course and sat through two days of intensive training. Interestingly, the first thing they taught was how to study. It violated everything I had ever learned about preparation.

You were told to read out loud while writing down what you were reading! The principle is that your brain will learn and retain more if you are using more of your senses. (Reading out-load, while you are writing is actually using four of your senses).

The other experience was when I gave my first talk in front of about 80 people. I knew the material. But by rehearsing out loud the talk, I became comfortable with the material. I cemented in my mind how I would present that material.

So, if you can cement in your mind what you *do* want, you can also experience the pain of cementing things in your brain that you don't want there. Like, "I am starting to feel a cold coming on...." And other such incredibly unproductive statements. Its' bad enough to think it, but...*Be very careful what you say out loud!!*

A quick review of this chapter. You must tend to your seed and your crop to assure a harvest. You cannot allow the weeds of *'failure thought'* to enter your brain. Success is an attitude and takes full time work and concentration. It takes work at controlling and programming. There is no luck involved with people who are successful. They have programmed and controlled their future through their minds and attitudes.

Take responsibility!! That's correct. Be able to accept that you are the reason you are where you are presently - by your thoughts, your actions, (your speech), your attitude, and your preparedness. Belly up and take responsibility for you. Avoid the blame game.

And don't be lazy! Really, why should you have to be motivated by some external source or person to move you forward? Of course, we all want to say we are the greatest and rely on excuses to let us off the hook. Rather than put yourself down, look at what you have or haven't done in the pursuit of your goals and dreams and make the proper corrections.

G Suit & Helmet Not Required!!

"The truest wisdom is a resolute determination." Napoleon

Have you ever watched a video of a missile launched from a plane at the target? If it is a moving target, as life is, then the missile is constantly leading the target slightly and is also constantly making the corrections necessary to hit the target. A splash on the target is a result of hundreds of course corrections. You are not a missile, but you should be....

It does matter at what you are aiming. Be sure of the target, lock in on it, and then with total and absolute concentration and focus, stay moving towards the goal. Make the corrections, but never give up on the prize.

Holistic life involves many aspects. Time and space do not allow for details to all of them here. But I must mention part of effective 'growing it'. It is a concentration on being involved in all areas of your life. Any one of them can cause you to fail:

Health: This is an unbelievably easy deal. Really. I do not comprehend the amount of time and money people spend on taking care of the body God has given you. When you are injured and/or sick, this becomes a major focus in your life, and all else is relegated to minor importance. So, work on this proactively to prevent a lack of good health to rule your day.

Two main *health secrets* are:

1) Be proactive (not reactive). Do not let a doctor figure out your needs. Read about what a healthy regimen entails. It includes attitude, nutrition and spinal alignment. (*Fighter Pilot in the Kitchen - A Cookbook for Every Man*.)

2) Stay in motion. Of course you can go to a gym or work-out facility. There is nothing wrong with doing that. However, if you don't feel you have the time necessary, at least start everyday with a stretching routine. Do this within the first five or

ten minutes after arising. This will help you get alert, focused, drastically improve your morning attitude and prevent injuries. Plus, you will gently increase your metabolic and heart rate to maintain a healthy weight and shape. Walk or ride a bike 4 or more times per week.

Relationships: The health of your relationships will have a huge positive or negative influence on whatever it is you are attempting to do. Again, be proactive. Never reactive. It is very hard to get back to a place where you are comfortable, if you let this get away from you.

1) *Financial concerns:* You can't allow yourself to be distracted. If you can't deal with the major effects of the financial concerns in your life you will be destroyed on the way to your target. You cannot allow yourself to get behind. But if you do, you must fight your way back to the top. It is inevitable that we experience the tides of life. Sometimes, the tide is in, sometimes, it is out. You try to minimize when the tide is out and maximize when it is in. But, no matter what else, you have to battle your way back. Remember it is fruitless to participate in the blame game, or to justify that everyone else is in the same boat, or

that there are good reasons and excuses. It is totally immaterial. Just don't accept the present as your permanent reality.

2) *Spiritual*: Your emotional life is completely intertwined with your whole or holistic well being. A focused energy towards a daily and weekly routine in worship and reflection are essential. Again, it is crucial to be proactive instead of reactive.

"Can you imagine what I would do if I could do all I can?"
Sun Tzu

These few items in no way constitute an entire list. But each of these are major areas of life and must be touched on briefly. It is essential to take this abbreviated list and expand your thoughts on what is required in action for you to work on these items.

Earlier, in the chapter - 'planting it', I wrote about the process of goal setting. Much is written and lectured regarding goal setting. Remember though, a goal is like the target. Why would you consider launching a couple of expensive missiles at a non-target? Why would you shoot at something that doesn't exist?

It is crazy to me how much time and energy some people take at getting ready to get ready. It is comparable to me like those people endlessly going to school. School is not wrong.

Come on though. You really have no reason to go to school unless it is satisfy prerequisites for a predetermined goal. Just to endlessly attend school, spending money and time on the pursuit of a 'piece of paper' in the hopes of maybe ascertaining what it is you want to do in life is madness!

Many of you probably can point fingers at your own life and know what I am talking about. We are less than certain about setting the priorities in our lives to determine our end result. So someone tells us to get out there and get a degree and then we go looking for a job. And all this without ever even knowing how much the job will pay, where we will live, or how much time we will have left over to 'live' our life.

So, I want to hit it again, in case you didn't do it when I hit on it earlier. Stop now, if you haven't done so already and forget about a job that you might have considered. Stop and determine what you want your life to look like. Do this and consider the endless hours spent every day doing something that is not rewarding or fulfilling.

Areas to consider at any age or station in life:

1) Spiritual

2) Family

3) Income

4) Longevity and health

5) Leisure

6) Volunteering

7) And finally, rewards of work. I am sure you have heard it said that your perfect job or business

would be one that you would truly do without pay. Because it means enough to you that you want to do it - without regard to what it is.

"A man who wants to lead the orchestra must turn his back on the crowd." Max Lucado

Jot down some thoughts about this target/goal, so you may begin firing your missiles at the target/prize and make the corrections to do what *you* will - not what is left over for you to do.

Again, take responsibility. Don't make excuses. If you wanted to be a fighter pilot, why didn't you? Why don't you? Is it really too late?

When flying as a flight lead, there were many elements that went into the mission. First, we would get scheduled a flight time, as well as the number of jets that would be in the flight. Next, we would be given the names for the each assigned aircraft. They would generally be assigned to a 'position' based on their experience level.

"When it is obvious that the goals cannot be reached, don't adjust the goals, adjust the action steps." Confucius

Lead was always number one. Not necessarily because he had the most rank or flight time. The leader that day might be gaining experience with other more experienced pilots in the formation. Typically, there were two elements of two planes.

www.philipbrewer.com

Each element had responsibility within the formation of four.

'Lead' would also accept the assigned mission for the day's flight. In peace time, this would usually be a simulated combat flight to a bombing range. Sometimes it would also involve other, dissimilar types of aircraft.

In a Search and Rescue (SAR) mission, this would involve a refueling tanker (the gas station in the sky), 'jolly green' rescue helicopters, and other fighter support. A forward air controller (FAC) would designate (identify and point out) the survivor. The SAR leader, also known as "Sandy" would locate and authenticate the survivor on the ground in hostile enemy territory.

This was a very complex mission, and it would take enormous amounts of time and energy to plan. However, there usually wasn't any time. The time of the survivor to stay 'free' of capture was minimal.

Therefore, the success of the mission meant to always be ready. Preparedness was the key. Even so, essential elements of the pre-flight briefing would entail times, fuel considerations, ordinances, weather related and hostile forces scenarios, as well as abort procedures, low fuel and safe flight areas. You would plan and discuss the applicable rules of engagement, also known as ROI, for the mission type, minimum flight altitudes, call signs, etc.

No matter how well planned you might be, the fluidity of the mission and the exigencies of the ever-changing battle plan forced a flight to constantly be able to adapt and change, always within the confines of the discipline of the leader.

"Any idea, plan, or purpose may be placed in the mind through repetition of thought." Napoleon Hill

www.philipbrewer.com

G Suit & Helmet Not Required!!

In all cases, you couldn't just order people around. You had to exude confidence, make rational decisions and keep everything flowing forward. In life, we get the luxury of thinking that we can always back off, take a break, sit down, relax, entertain ourselves.

In reality, can you really do this, when there is so much at stake? You should be constantly thinking of how you can fulfill your mission plan - hourly, daily, weekly, monthly, and yearly.

However, even if you have a well-written plan, you still need to be flexible. Flexibility in flight was as important as being flexible in arriving at the successful achievement of your goals.

A very important aspect to the flight's success went into this extensive planning. It was a very focused and busy time before the flight, one that made the flight a success or less than a success on the mission. Or even disaster! If you had the luxury of planning the flight over several days, that would also allow for even more studying and planning.

Eventually, the scheduled time would occur when action had to commence. The planning was over. It was time to take off and go towards the mission. Taking each of these same aspects is very similar in life to what we need to do. Your life's planning and then movement towards your dreams and goals.

"When written in Chinese, the word 'crisis' is composed of two characters. One represents danger and the other represents opportunity." John F Kennedy

In life, there is this comparison. There is a time of intense focus. My challenge to you is to focus with intense concentration, several times each week. Do this as if you were preparing for a flight, allowing a one hour block of time.

Focus completely, without the distractions inherent in your office or work environment that might pull you away. If it is at home, prepare your work area to be free of distractions.

If it is in a job or office environment, put a 'Do Not Disturb' sign on your cubicle. The important thing is to mentally and physically engage your creative energy towards the mission or goal you have set.

Secret #4 Harvest Your Crop

What is meant by harvesting your crop? Think of a farmer on a combine out cutting and threshing, or whatever it is they do. They leave the crop sitting in the fields for a while. Eventually, the farmer comes and collects the harvest. The farmer puts it in some sort of storage facility, and eventually, it goes off to market.

So, in this book, what have we accomplished? We have touched on items of the planting aspect of a project. From identifying and planting your seed, to growing it, and now finally to the harvest. The activity in life never stops.

We should remember that part of what is accomplished in harvesting a farm crop, is the retention of seed for the next planting. So, in reality, it is not an end, but a cycle oriented around a new beginning.

Picking the best seed from your life, selling off the harvest of the rest of your 'crop', and then preparing the ground for the next year is an essential element of your existence. Look at what you have accomplished in the pursuit of your goals, re-examine the good things and bad, and then reset your new goals.

"My poor dad would say, 'I can't afford it,' while my rich dad would say, 'How can I afford it?" Robert Kiyosaki

When setting your new goals, be careful not to constrict or contract your mind set. Occasionally, when we have the inevitable set backs, the temptation is to ease back into the 'known' comfort zone. We might include 'tightening our belt' financially. While it is definitely responsible to attempt to live within our means, and for sure our budget, be very careful that you don't go backwards in your thinking.

"Dreams come true. Without that possibility, nature would not incite us to have them." John Updike

Attack life! The best defense in my opinion is a strong, powerful and even willful offense. Sure, don't go purchase a Bentley if you can only presently afford a nice Buick. But don't back out of your Buick into an even lesser car to attempt to 'afford' life.

No matter when or where you are in your life, whatever you have or have not accomplished, it is always time to stop on occasion and evaluate the condition in which you find yourself. Then, prepare yourself anew for the next set of challenges and get excited about going forward.

Concluding remarks: In the Bible, there is a very powerful message relayed by one of the writers. "Give thanks in all things." When you think of this, you should never get upset or angry about anything. There is a definite benefit, seen or not, which has occurred.

While writing these last few pages, I went to the Phoenix airport to pick up a very special person, and when I went back to where the car was parked, I simply couldn't find it. We were delayed late into the evening for at least forty minutes while I stumbled around looking and finally asking for help.

I am absolutely sure of the message. There was some benefit that occurred. Maybe in our relationship. Maybe it was in preparing myself to not do that again. Or, maybe a major accident was avoided.

All day long, life hands us little opportunities. Sometimes, they look like insurmountable obstacles and hurdles. Some of them hurt us and mar us emotionally. Yet, we need to see each of these for what they are, and allow them the benefit of moving into our life in the most positive way possible.

In doing this, we are preparing our fields for the seeds we will plant in them, and this will determine the new crop and its health and the future foundations of our well-being and success in life!!

Finally, make your life the one you want it to be. And always bear in mind, you are the one ultimately in control!!

www.philipbrewer.com

G Suit & Helmet Not Required!!

Contact

Any time: *www.philipbrewer.com*

Other books by Phil:

"Changes the Book - A Remembrance of Sorts"

"Fighter Pilot in the Kitchen - A Cookbook for Every Man"

Phil is available for coaching and speaking engagements.

Reviews and Endorsements:

"Phil has shown great success in the projects he has undertaken and is very successful as a business owner." *Gary Brown, Owner, Brown & Associates.*

"I've known Phil for over 15 years and he is one of the most trustworthy people I have ever met. He is an excellent networker and instantly connects with people he meets. He is one of those people who never meets a stranger. I have worked with him on several projects over the years, and if I ever had the opportunity again, I would do it in a heartbeat." *Russell Landry, CEO/President, Landry Home Health Supply, Inc.*

"Phil is an active, bright and good friend, who is always looking for innovations and best business strategies. Thanks" *Pedram Owtad, IT, Prologic Technology Group LLC.*

"Phil has motivated many people to achieve above and beyond anything they felt they could achieve through his mentoring and leadership activities. My view of what I can accomplish has been greatly enhanced by my relationship with Phil." *John Thelen, IT Development Manager, Prisma Graphic Corporation.*

www.philipbrewer.com

G Suit & Helmet Not Required!!

"Being able to utilize the help of real-world people and their experiences is paramount to personal growth. And sometimes, all we need is a bit of common sense and straight talk to get us there. Phil's book offers just that, within an exciting scope of expertise. His personal anecdotes, though mainly specific to military/aviation, are relatable, and their lessons warrant great value for anyone." *Rachel Beard, screenwriter.*

"Phil is an incredibly inspiring figure who stands out starkly against the bleak landscape of modernity. In this book, he takes timeless wisdom to new heights for any reader. The result is an absolute joy, whether you need a shove or just a nudge toward positive thinking." *Mark Brewer Founding Partner, Brewer & Pritchard PC www.bplaw.com*

"What an inspiring book! I like the pace and all the allusions to flying. Like the way you lifted off with.... 'breaking free of the bonds of gravity we begin our climb .... You've got many more memorable quotes: 'The Rules are a good place to hide if you don't have a better idea and the talent to execute it.' Or - 'One of the beautiful things about a single pilot aircraft is the quality of the social experience.' ...."The advice is right on-- recognizing achievements regardless of their size and not letting a little put-down throw one off course; don't allow the weeds of failure thoughts, etc... The crab in the bucket analogy is absolutely true." *William Cates author <u>The Unlimited Salad Bar</u> of and other entertaining books.*

"Get this book! Thanks Phil, for your support & service to our Country." *Coach Ron Tunick, author of <u>The Thinking Room</u>. President of Nations Transaction Services & radio personality.*

"A short and clear exposition of the principles and practices of a successful jet pilot and how to apply those practices and principles to all of life. It will help you get off the ground and fly." William Ophuls, author of <u>Immoderate Greatness, Why Civilizations Fail, Sane Polity, A Pattern Language, Plato's Revenge: Politics in the Age of Ecology and many fine other books</u>.

www.philipbrewer.com

G Suit & Helmet Not Required!!

Phil Brewer - Fighter Pilot, Business Man, Entrepreneur, Consultant, Author, Publisher, Coach and Speaker

Major Accomplishments:

Business:

Owner of *www.Amazon.com* kitchen product business, *www.FighterPilotintheKitchen.com*

Past President - International Orthodox Christian Charity, operating 24 retail bookshops located throughout the United Kingdom.

Developer for a Medical Distribution & Medical Office service business.

Owner/developer for a Network Marketing business responsible for training & coaching hundreds of aspiring and new franchise business owners.

Organizer, speaker trainer for major events attended by thousands.

District Manager Major Fast Food Restaurant Chain.

Owner/developer for an 9 store restaurant chain.

Professional Pilot Roles:

Combat trained attack/fighter pilot, flying the A7D Corsair II, and later the A10A Warthog.

USAF Formal Course Instructor Pilot, A10A.

Civilian contract instructor pilot in the Royal Saudi Air Force in F15C aircraft simulator, Taif, Saudi Arabia Pilot. Range Safety Supervisor, Khamis Mushayt, Saudi Arabia.

Captain on an international airline.

www.philipbrewer.com

G Suit & Helmet Not Required!!

Phil received his Bachelor's Degree in History and Aerospace Studies Southern Illinois University, Edwardsville Campus.

Phil is married, has a son and 3 grandchildren.

my wonderful friend and wife, Monica.

"A day without laughter is a day wasted." Charlie Chaplin

www.philipbrewer.com